D1717085

21.95

21.95

APR   2019

SAN FRANCISCO
GIANTS
STARS, STATS, HISTORY, AND MORE!
BY JIM GIGLIOTTI

The Child's World®
childsworld.com

Published by The Child's World®
1980 Lookout Drive • Mankato, MN 56003-1705
800-599-READ • www.childsworld.com

ISBN 9781503828377
LCCN 2018944852

Printed in the United States of America
PAO2392

Photo Credits:
Cover: Joe Robbins (2).
Inside: AP Images: 8, Mark J. Terrill 11, 19, 23;
Dreamstime.com: Richard Coences 12, EBud 20;
Library of Congress: 29; Newscom: Mark Faulkner/MCT
4, Terry Schmitt/UPI 17; Joe Robbins: 7, 24;
Shutterstock: Eric Broder Van Dyke 14, PhotoWorks 27.

About the Author

Jim Gigliotti has worked for
the University of Southern
California's athletic
department, the Los Angeles
Dodgers, and the National
Football League. He is now an
author who has written more
than 80 books, mostly for
young readers, on a variety
of topics.

On the Cover

Main photo: Star Giants catcher
Buster Posey
Inset: Hall of Fame legend
Willie Mays

CONTENTS

Go, Giants! 5

Who Are the Giants? 6

Where They Came From 9

Who They Play 10

Where They Play 13

The Baseball Field 14

Big Days 16

Tough Days 18

Meet the Fans! 21

Heroes Then 22

Heroes Now 25

Gearing Up 26

Team Stats 28

Glossary 30

Find Out More 31

Index 32

GO, GIANTS!

The Giants have a long history. They have been playing for more than 130 years! They have a great present, too! The team has been one of baseball's best of the 2000s. In 2010, the Giants won the **World Series**. It was their first championship since 1954. Then they won again in 2012 . . . and again in 2014! Each year, Giants fans pack the team's beautiful ballpark. They hope to see yet another title!

◄ *Buster Posey holds up the World Series trophy after the Giants won in 2010.*

WHO ARE THE GIANTS?

The Giants play in the National League (NL). That group is part of Major League Baseball (MLB). MLB also includes the American League (AL). There are 30 teams in MLB. The winner of the NL plays the winner of the AL in the World Series. The Giants have won the World Series eight times. They were champs five times when the team played in New York. They have won three titles in San Francisco.

First baseman Brandon Belt gets ready to make a play for the Giants. ➤

WHERE THEY CAME FROM

The Giants began playing in New York in 1883. They were first called the Gothams. In 1886, the Gothams **manager**, Jim Mutrie, was inspired by the team's play. He called his players "my giants." The name stuck. The Giants played in New York through 1957. In 1958, the team moved to San Francisco. The Dodgers also moved that year from Brooklyn to Los Angeles. They were the first big-league teams on the West Coast.

◄ *Hall of Fame pitcher Carl Hubbell played for the New York Giants from 1928 to 1943.*

WHO THEY PLAY

The Giants play 162 games each season. For the team's fans, the biggest games are against the Los Angeles Dodgers. The Giants and Dodgers have been **rivals** since they played in New York. The teams don't like each other very much! Both teams now play in the NL West Division. The division also includes the Arizona Diamondbacks, the Colorado Rockies, and the San Diego Padres.

Mac Williamson scored for the Giants as they ➤
battled the rival Dodgers in 2018.

11

WHERE THEY PLAY

The Giants play their home games at AT&T Park. The stadium opened in 2000. It has a huge baseball glove and soda bottle beyond the left-field stands! Inside the soda bottle is a slide. Kids love to go down the slide during Giants' games. The park was built on the San Francisco **waterfront**. Home runs over the right-field seats land in the water! Those homers are called "splash hits"!

◄ *A statue of superstar Willie Mays stands outside AT&T Park.*

THE BASEBALL FIELD

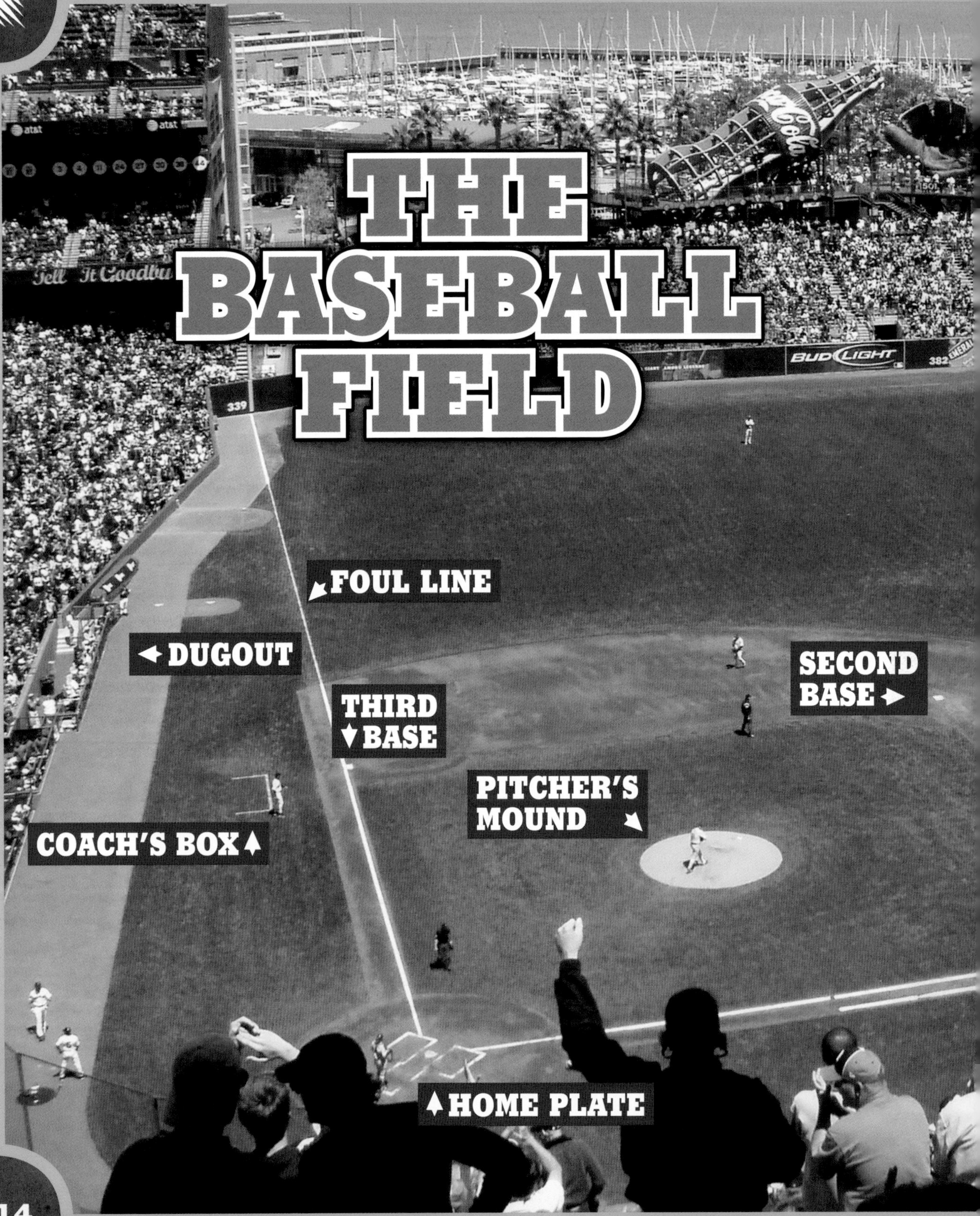

FOUL LINE

DUGOUT

SECOND BASE

THIRD BASE

PITCHER'S MOUND

COACH'S BOX

HOME PLATE

OUTFIELD
INFIELD
FOUL LINE
FIRST BASE
TOYOTA
SAFEWAY
Budweiser
CHW
Health Services
HOME RUN
744
TALK TO CHUCK
charles
SCHWAB
YAHOO!
404
399
VISA
Bank of America

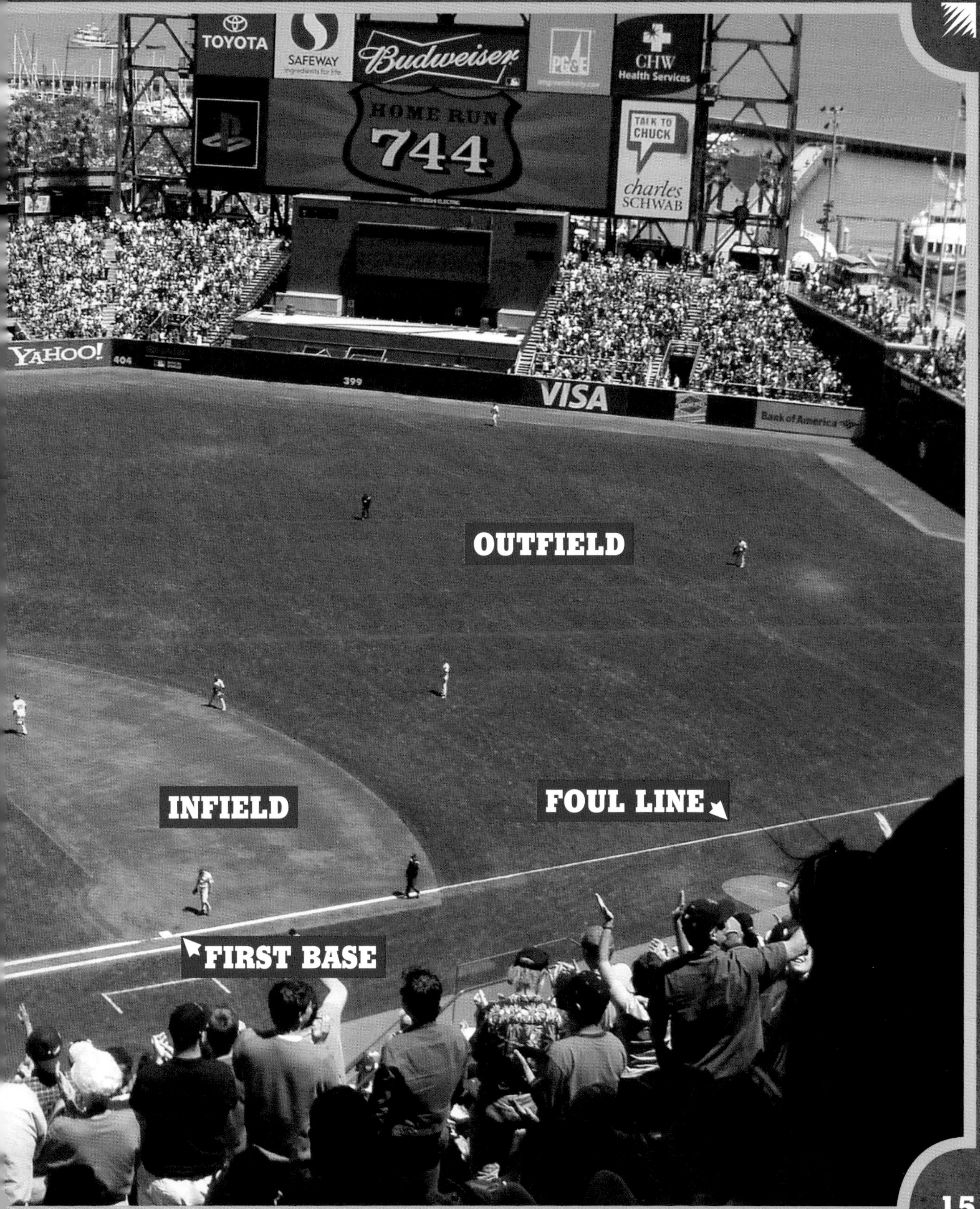

BIG DAYS

In 1951, Bobby Thomson of the Giants hit the "Shot Heard 'Round the World." The home run beat the Dodgers in a **playoff** game. It is one of baseball's most famous moments. Here are a few other big days for the Giants.

1961—Superstar Willie Mays hit a home run in the first inning at Milwaukee. He was just warming up. He homered again in the third inning. And in the sixth. And in the eighth. His four home runs tied the MLB record. The Giants won 14–4.

Madison Bumgarner was the MVP of the ➤
2014 World Series for the Giants.

1989—The Giants and Cubs were tied 1–1 in Game 5 of the NL playoffs. Will Clark lined a single up the middle. Two runs scored. The Giants were on their way to the World Series.

2014—The Giants played Kansas City in the World Series. Madison Bumgarner pitched the Giants to a win in Game 1. He tossed a **shutout** in Game 5. Amazingly, he pitched as a **reliever** only two days later. The Giants won 3–2. They were champs again!

TOUGH DAYS

Here are a few moments Giants fans don't want to remember!

1924—Game 7 of the World Series was tied 3–3 in the 12th inning. A Washington player hit a ground ball. It looked like a sure double play. But the ball hit a pebble. It took a huge hop over Giants infielder Fred Lindstrom's head. The winning run scored.

1962—The Giants trailed the New York Yankees 1–0 in the bottom of the ninth inning of Game 7 of the World Series. Giants slugger Willie McCovey hit a screaming line drive . . . right at the second baseman. The Yankees won the game . . . and the Series.

2002—It looked like the Giants would finally win a title for San Francisco. They led the Anaheim Angels three games to two in the World Series. And they led Game 6 5–0. But the Angels stormed back to win the game. Anaheim won again the next night to take the series.

▼ *"Willie Mac" was nearly a World Series hero in 1962.*

MEET THE FANS!

Giants fans are some of the most **devoted** in baseball. For many years, they braved cold and windy weather at Candlestick Park. The team played in that stadium for 40 years. Today, the fans love AT&T Park. It's not as windy there! Fans have views of San Francisco Bay. In one stretch, the Giants sold out every home game they played from 2010 to 2017. That was 530 games in a row!

◄ *Some Giants fans wait in boats behind the left-field wall. They hope to catch home runs that fly into the water!*

HEROES THEN

When the Giants played in New York, they had many Hall of Fame stars. Two of the best were pitcher Christy Mathewson and outfielder Willie Mays. Mays said "Say hey!" to greet people. So reporters called him the "Say Hey Kid." First baseman Willie McCovey was called "Stretch." He was a fan favorite who hit many long home runs. No one in baseball history hit more homers than outfielder Barry Bonds. He played 15 seasons for the Giants.

Willie Mays holds up one baseball for each ➤
of the four homers he hit in a 1961 game.

HEROES NOW

Giants fans will always remember pitcher Madison Bumgarner for the 2014 World Series. But "MadBum" has been one of baseball's best for several years. Buster Posey is an All-Star catcher and was the 2012 NL MVP. Posey is a great hitter. He's strong behind the plate, too. Brandon Belt is a good-fielding first baseman with a sweet swing. The tall star is nicknamed "Baby Giraffe." Some Giants fans come to the games wearing a giraffe hat!

◀ *Buster Posey is one of baseball's best all-around catchers.*

GEARING UP

Baseball players wear team uniforms. On defense, they wear leather gloves to catch the ball. As batters, they wear hard helmets. This protects them from pitches. Batters hit the ball with long wood bats. Each player chooses his own size of bat. Catchers have the toughest job. They wear a lot of protection.

THE BASEBALL

The outside of the Major League baseball is made from cow leather. Two leather pieces shaped like 8's are stitched together. There are 108 stitches of red thread. These stitches help players grip the ball. Inside, the ball has a small center of cork and rubber. Hundreds of feet of yarn are tightly wound around this center.

CHEST PROTECTOR ➤

WRIST ◄ BAND

CATCHER'S MASK AND HELMET ↘

CATCHER'S MITT ↖

SHIN GUARDS ➤

CATCHER'S GEAR

TEAM STATS

Here are some of the all-time career records for the Giants. All these stats are through the 2018 regular season.

HOME RUNS

Willie Mays	646
Barry Bonds	586

RBI

Mel Ott	1,860
Willie Mays	1,859

BATTING AVERAGE

Bill Terry	.341
Mike Donlin	.333

STOLEN BASES

Mike Tiernan	428
George Davis	357

WINS

Christy Mathewson	372
Carl Hubbell	253

SAVES

Robb Nen	206
Rod Beck	199

Christy Mathewson played for the Giants from 1900 ➤
to 1916. He is tied for third all-time in wins.

STRIKEOUTS

Christy Mathewson	2,504
Juan Marichal	2,281

MATHEWSON, N. Y. NAT'L

GLOSSARY

devoted (dee-VOTE-ed) very loyal

manager (MAN-uh-jer) in baseball, the person who is in charge of the team on the field

playoff (PLAY-off) a game or series played between top teams to determine who moves ahead

reliever (ruh-LEEV-er) a pitcher who does not start the game

rivals (RYE-vuhls) two people or groups competing for the same thing

shutout (SHUT-owt) a game in which the starting pitcher finishes the whole game without giving up a run

waterfront (WAHT-er-frunt) land or buildings alongside a body of water

World Series (WURLD SEER-eez) the championship of Major League Baseball, played between the winners of the AL and NL

FIND OUT MORE

IN THE LIBRARY

Fishman, Jon M. *Buster Posey (Amazing Athletes)*. Minneapolis, MN: Lerner Publishing Group, 2016.

Tometich, Annabelle. *Superstars of the San Francisco Giants (Pro Sports Superstars)*. Mankato, MN: Amicus, 2014.

Williams, Doug. *12 Reasons to Love the San Francisco Giants*. Mankato, MN: 12-Story Library, 2016.

ON THE WEB

Visit our website for links about the
San Francisco Giants:
childsworld.com/links

Note to Parents, Teachers, and Librarians: We routinely verify our web links to make sure they are safe and active sites. So encourage your readers to check them out!

INDEX

Anaheim Angels, 19

Arizona Diamondbacks, 10

AT&T Park, 13, 21

Belt, Brandon, 6, 25

Bonds, Barry, 22, 28

Brooklyn Dodgers, 9, 16

Bumgarner, Madison, 16, 17, 25

Candlestick Park, 21

Chicago Cubs, 17

Clark, Will, 17

Colorado Rockies, 10

gear, 26

Hubbell, Carl, 9

Kansas City Royals, 17

Lindstrom, Fred, 18

Los Angeles Dodgers, 9, 10

Mathewson, Christy, 22, 28, 29

Mays, Willie, 13, 16, 22, 28

McCovey, Willie, 18, 19, 22

Mutrie, Jim, 9

National League, 6, 10

New York Gothams, 9

New York Yankees, 18

Posey, Buster, 5, 25

San Francisco Bay, 13, 21

San Diego Padres, 10

Thomson, Bobby, 16

Washington Senators, 18

Williamson, Mac, 10

World Series, 5, 6, 16, 17, 18, 19, 25